A Practical Guide to Asylum Support and Judicial Review

Stephen Tawiah is a practising barrister at 33 Bedford Row Chambers and has practised in public law and immigration and asylum law since qualifying, having been attracted to the work because of his strong belief and support for upholding human rights and promoting good administration. Stephen has worked extensively in the pro-bono legal sector, particularly in various law centres.

A Practical Guide to Asylum Support and Judicial Review

Stephen Tawiah

Barrister, Lincoln's Inn

Law Brief Publishing

Published 2025 by Law Brief Publishing, an imprint of Law Brief Publishing Ltd
30 The Parks
Minehead
Somerset
TA24 8BT

www.lawbriefpublishing.com

Paperback: 978-1-916698-66-6

PREFACE

The purpose of this book is to provide a straightforward account of asylum support, and the role that judicial review plays in this developing area of law. In many respects, this area can be considered as the interface between immigration and asylum, community care and administrative law. There has been a series of judgments in the higher courts of England and Wales which have provided guidance on the relevant standards and duties which apply in this area.

Despite being a developing area of law, asylum support regularly courts public attention and is a subject of discourse in all parts of the United Kingdom. This in part can be attributed to the fact that asylum support relates to asylum seekers.

Refugees and asylum seekers are subjects of charged political discussion in the UK. Particularly as political parties seek to adopt positions on refugees and asylum seekers that they believe will be politically amenable. Asylum support is an easy go-to topic for politicians. This can be explained by the numerous myths around this area. Also, the public can see the provision of asylum support. They see when a hotel is being used to accommodate asylum seekers; or when an ex-Ministry of Defence site has been turned into asylum support accommodation. But beyond what meets the physical eye, there is a complicated legal framework. Decision makers are required to grapple with the individual circumstances of individuals who have fled countries and are still adjusting to a new environment. There is no asylum support case which is the same.

The legislative framework in this area includes both international and domestic law. However, for our purposes the most relevant legislation is as follows: Immigration and Asylum Act 1999 (IAA 1999) and the Asylum Seekers (Reception Conditions) Regulations 2005 ('2005

Regs'). This area is also heavily influenced by government guidance and policy. These will be referred to throughout the book.

In this book, the areas of asylum support we will be focused on are section 95(1) IAA 1999, section 98(1) IAA 1999 and s4(2) IAA 1999. Asylum support is not limited to these forms of support. There are other areas which are relevant. However, this book does not seek to be a treatise on asylum support. The areas covered by this book are sufficient to provide a foundation for the wider area of asylum support.

Furthermore, a significant section of this book is dedicated to the practice of judicial review in the context of asylum support. The basics of the judicial review process are explained for those who are new to the area. However, the book seeks to provide a practical understanding of how asylum support cases make their way through the judicial review process. Lastly, the book analyses two recent High Court judgments that address key asylum support issues. This is with the aim of giving readers an understanding of how the courts have grappled with this area, and the sort of matters that lawyers must turn their mind to.

In conclusion, I hope this book can be of benefit to all readers and students.

The law stated in this book is believed to be accurate and up to date as at 1st December 2024.

Stephen Tawiah
December 2024

CONTENTS

Chapter One	Section 95(1) Support of the Immigration and Asylum Act 1999	1
	Section 98(1) Support of the Immigration and Asylum Act 1999	34
Chapter Two	Section 4(2) Support of the Immigration and Asylum Act 1999	37
Chapter Three	Judicial Review and Asylum Support	55
Chapter Four	Key Recent Judgments in the Area of Asylum Support	75

CHAPTER ONE

SECTION 95(1) SUPPORT OF THE IMMIGRATION AND ASYLUM ACT 1999

1. We will address in this chapter the provision of accommodation and financial support to asylum-seekers and their dependants in England and Wales by the Home Office, under section 95(1) (hereinafter referred to as s95(1)) of the Immigration and Asylum Act 1999 (IAA 1999).

Who is eligible for s95(1) support?

2. Under s95(1) of the IAA 1999, the Secretary of State may provide, or arrange for the provision of support (which may take the form of accommodation and subsistence or subsistence only) for:

    - asylum-seekers or dependants of asylum-seekers;

    - who appear to the secretary of state to be destitute or likely to become destitute within a 'prescribed period'.

3. We will now turn to specifically look at the terms which make up the eligibility criteria. The significance of these terms is that entitlement to support can often turn on whether or not a specific term is satisfied. It is also noteworthy that some of these terms may have alternative meanings elsewhere in the immigration and asylum legal architecture. Therefore, it is necessary that the specific definitions of these terms in the context of asylum support are understood.

Asylum-seeker

4. Section 94 of the IA 1999, outlines various definitions relevant to the legal framework for asylum support. In particular, it defines 'asylum-seeker' as:

> "*a person who is not under 18 and has made a claim for asylum which has been recorded by the Secretary of State but which has not been determined*".[1]

What is a claim for asylum?

5. Section 94 also defines the term 'claim for asylum' in the following terms:

> "*a claim that it would be contrary to the United Kingdom's obligations under the Refugee Convention, or under Article 3 of the Human Rights Convention, for the claimant to be removed from, or required to leave, the United Kingdom*"[2].

6. The reference to an asylum seeker being a person who is not under 18 and has *made* a claim would suggest that the person is not a minor, and there has been a positive assertion of rights under the Refugee Convention and/or Article 3 of the ECHR.

What is a claim 'which has been recorded'?

7. The stage at which a person reports an asylum claim to the Home Office, is normally the stage at which the matter is recorded. Depending on the context, persons may claim asylum on arrival in the UK or at a later stage when they are already in the UK. The

---

1 s94(1) IAA 1999

2 s94(1) IAA 1999

procedure for making an asylum claim begins with making a claim at a designated place. Section 14(2) of the Nationality and Borders Act 2022 defines a designated place as[3]:

(a) a place identified in a notice published by the Secretary of State as an asylum intake unit;

(b) a removal centre (within the meaning of section 147 of the Immigration and Asylum Act 1999);

(c) a port (within the meaning of section 33 of the Immigration Act 1971);

(d) a place where there is a person present who, for the purposes of the immigration rules, is authorised to accept an asylum claim on behalf of the Secretary of State;

(e) a place to which the claimant has been directed by the Secretary of State or an immigration officer to make the claim.

8. However, the above general position only covers the situation relating to an initial claim for asylum. This matter is more nuanced when considering the issue of further submissions and whether they amount to a fresh claim for asylum. The question which ultimately arises is: when do further submissions for asylum amount to a 'claim for asylum which has been recorded'?

9. The starting point is to first understand what constitutes a fresh asylum claim. This is dealt with under paragraph 353 of the Immigration Rules, which states as follows[4]:

---

3 s14(2) NBA 2002

4 Paragraph 353 of the Immigration Rules

Fresh Claims

353. When a human rights or protection claim has been refused or withdrawn or treated as withdrawn under paragraph 333C of these Rules and any appeal relating to that claim is no longer pending, the decision maker will consider any further submissions and, if rejected, will then determine whether they amount to a fresh claim. The submissions will amount to a fresh claim if they are significantly different from the material that has previously been considered. The submissions will only be significantly different if the content:

(i) had not already been considered; and

(ii) taken together with the previously considered material, created a realistic prospect of success, notwithstanding its rejection. This paragraph does not apply to claims made overseas.

10. Ultimately, when an initial asylum claim has been refused or withdrawn, the Secretary of State will consider any further submissions made by the Applicant (and if rejected) will assess whether they amount to a fresh claim. The Court of Appeal in *WM (Democratic Republic of Congo) v SSHD*[5] determined the test for further submissions amounting to a fresh claim is:

> "*The question is whether there is a realistic prospect that an immigration tribunal, equipped with the previous evidence and any new evidence could conclude that a further appeal against the refusal of a protection or human rights claim should be allowed*".

5 [2006] EWCA Civ 1495

It is only if this is satisfied that the Secretary of State will consider the content as significantly different".

11. The significance of this issue in the context of s95(1) eligibility is that the Home Office will not treat further submissions in support of a fresh claim for asylum as 'a claim recorded' until the Secretary of State assesses the further submissions to be a fresh claim within the meaning of paragraph 353 of the Immigration Rules.

12. The importance of this is that a person waiting for the Secretary of State to decide whether their further submissions amount to a fresh claim, will not be eligible for s95(1) support. The seminal case of *R (Nigatu) v SSHD*[6], has highlighted the importance of this issue. This case concerned the removal of asylum support from the claimant, in circumstances when he asserted that he was still entitled to such support. The Claimant had claimed asylum, that claim had been rejected by the Secretary of State, and his appeals and attempted statutory review of the refusal of leave to appeal to the Immigration Appeal Tribunal had all been dismissed. The Claimant submitted what he asserted was a fresh claim for asylum. The question before the Court was, essentially, whether that triggered the right to continue to receive asylum support under section 95(1) of the IAA 1999. The Court summarised the issue before it as follows[7]:

"*The question that therefore has to be answered is whether, in the circumstances of this case, and, more broadly, in circumstances where an asylum claim has been rejected and all appeal processes have been exhausted, the making of an application to the Secretary of State which is said to be a fresh claim is sufficient to require that support be continued because,*

6 [2004] EWHC 1806 (Admin)

7 [2004] EWHC 1806 (Admin) at para 1-2

as a matter of the true construction of section 94, the individual is an asylum seeker".

13. Collins J explained the appropriate approach to take in such matters[8]:

> 21.*It seems to me, in all the circumstances, that Miss Anderson's submissions are correct and that that is the true construction of this provision. There is a real difference between the situation when an initial claim for asylum is made and that when attempts are made to prevent removal following rejection and the exhaustion of all the appeal processes of that claim. The Secretary of State is indeed entitled to consider whether the representations made can properly be said to amount to a fresh claim so as to make the individual an asylum seeker. He will record that, and the evidence before me is that he does record that, when that preliminary decision is made and that the individual in question is notified when that happens. A record is made of that decision at that time.*
>
> *22.I am bound to say that Parliament must have meant something by requiring that the claim be recorded. One would have thought that if all that was meant was that it was received, that would have been said. Normally speaking, that will perhaps make no great difference because no system of sensible administration could work unless every application and every claim were recorded by someone when it was made. The question really turns on whether what was put before the Secretary of State can be said to have amounted to a claim for asylum. For the reasons that I have given, in my judgment, it does require the Secretary of State to decide the initial question*

8 [2004] EWHC 1806 (Admin) at para 21-22, 26

as to whether it should be regarded as a claim for asylum before any right to support within section 95 can arise.

....

26. Those are all matters that would have to be taken into account when considering the circumstances of any individual case. But I am satisfied that the making of what is asserted to be a fresh claim does not automatically trigger the right to continuing support as an asylum seeker. That only arises when the Secretary of State decides, obviously as soon as possible, that it can be properly regarded as a fresh claim, whether or not, as I said, in the end it succeeds.

14. Therefore, this position in Nigatu applies in cases relating to further submissions. The consequence of this is that an applicant for asylum support will be treated as an 'asylum-seeker' once the Secretary of State has recognised the further submissions as a fresh claim. This will constitute the point where their claim is considered as having been recorded.

What is a claim 'which has not been determined'?

15. For the purposes of eligibility for support under s.95(1), the recorded asylum claim must not have been determined. The relevant provision for understanding what a determined asylum claim means in this context is s.94(3) to s.94(4B)[9]:

(3) For the purposes of this Part, a claim for asylum is determined at the end of such period beginning—

9 S.94(3) and s94(4B) IA 1999

> *(a) on the day on which the Secretary of State notifies the claimant of his decision on the claim, or*
>
> *(b) if the claimant has appealed against the Secretary of State's decision, on the day on which the appeal is disposed of,*
>
> *as may be prescribed.*
>
> *(4) An appeal is disposed of when it is no longer pending for the purposes of the Immigration Acts or the Special Immigration Appeals Commission Act 1997.*
>
> *(4A) For the purposes of the definitions of "asylum-seeker" and "failed asylum-seeker", the circumstances in which a claim is determined or rejected include where the claim is declared inadmissible under section 80A or 80B of the Nationality, Immigration and Asylum Act 2002.*
>
> *(4B) But if a claim is—*
>
> *(a) declared inadmissible under section 80B of that Act, and*
>
> *(b) nevertheless considered by the Secretary of State in accordance subsection (7) of that section,*
>
> *the claim ceases to be treated as determined or rejected from the time of the decision to consider the claim.*

16. Therefore, in assessing if a claim has been determined, the following should be assessed:

    (a) Decision on the claim – accepted or refused by Secretary of State – s.94(3)(a)

    (b) Disposal of appeal – no longer pending

(c) Declared Inadmissible

Decision on the claim – accepted or refused by Secretary of State / Disposal of appeal – no longer pending

17. The starting point for this sub-section is to locate the relevant prescribed periods. The Home Office policy entitled '*Ceasing Section 95 Support Instruction*' version 3.0 outlines the various prescribed periods as follows[10]:

Prescribed periods

Applicants are entitled to receive asylum support for a prescribed period after they have been notified of the decision on their asylum application or after the day on which their appeal is disposed of (Section 94(3)(B) of the Immigration and Asylum Act 1999). This gives applicants the opportunity to make arrangements for additional accommodation and support or to make arrangements for their departure from the UK. For support purposes, an applicant ceases to be an asylum seeker after the prescribed period ends. The prescribed periods are:

- *28 days when the Secretary of State notifies the claimant of the decision to accept the asylum claim or the appeal is disposed of by being allowed; 30 days if the decision is served by post*

- *21 days in any other case*

There is no legislative power to provide support beyond the 21 or 28 day prescribed period. Therefore, support must be ceased at the end of the prescribed period unless the asylum seeker's

10 'Ceasing Section 95 Support' Instruction, version 3.0

household includes a dependent child, who was dependent on the asylum support application before the end of the prescribed period

18. Therefore, in relation to an accepted asylum claim, the claim is considered as having been determined 28 days from when the Secretary of State notifies the Claimant of the decision.

19. In relation to a rejected asylum claim which goes on to be allowed on appeal, the claim is considered as having been determined 28 days from the day on which the appeal was allowed.

20. In relation to a rejected asylum claim which goes on to be dismissed on appeal, the claim is considered as having been determined 21 days from the day on which the appeal was dismissed. The same principle applies if the Claimant does not exercise the right to appeal.

21. In relation to an appeal, section 94(4) indicates that an appeal is disposed of "*when it is no longer pending for the purposes of the Immigration Acts or the Special Immigration Appeals Commission Act 1997.*"

22. For our purposes, it is sufficient to acknowledge that under section 82(1) of the NIAA 2002, a person may appeal to the First-tier Tribunal (Immigration and Asylum Chamber) where the Secretary of State has refused their protection or human rights claim. There are circumstances where the Secretary of State may refuse a protection claim and also certify the claim so as to not carry an in-country right of appeal to the FTT. For the purposes of this discussion, it is unnecessary to address this point here.

23. S.11 and 13 of the Tribunals, Courts and Enforcement Act 2007 also provide a Claimant with rights of appeal to the Upper Tribunal and then the Court of Appeal.

24. Section 104 of the NIAA 2002, describes a pending appeal in the following terms[11]:

104 Pending appeal

(1) An appeal under section 82(1) is pending during the period—

(a) beginning when it is instituted, and

(b) ending when it is finally determined, withdrawn or abandoned (or when it lapses under section 99).

(2) An appeal under section 82(1) is not finally determined for the purpose of subsection (1)(b) while—

(a) an application for permission to appeal under section 11 or 13 of the Tribunals, Courts and Enforcement Act 2007 could be made or is awaiting determination,

(b) permission to appeal under either of those sections has been granted and the appeal is awaiting determination, or

(c) an appeal has been remitted under section 12 or 14 of that Act and is awaiting determination.

25. In short, this would suggest that until an Appellant is appeal rights exhausted, they still have a pending appeal.

---

[11] s104 of the NIAA 2002

What is claim that has been 'declared inadmissible'?

26. A claim is also treated as determined where it has been declared inadmissible. The relevant provisions when assessing this issue of inadmissibility can be found in s80A and 80B of NIAA 2002.

27. First, s80A makes it a requirement for the Secretary of State to declare an asylum claim made by an EU national as inadmissible, except where there are 'exceptional circumstances'. The definition of the phrase 'exceptional circumstances' is outlined in s80A(5).

28. Second, s80B permits the Secretary of State to declare inadmissible an asylum claim made by a person who has a 'connection to a safe third State', which is one where the applicant's life or liberty will not be threatened on any of the grounds protected by the Refugee Convention, where they will not be sent on to another state in contravention of the Refugee Convention or ECHR Article 3, and where they may apply to be recognised as a refugee. An applicant will have a 'connection' with such a state where the criteria in NIAA 2022 s80C are satisfied. In very broad terms, the criteria in NIAA 2022 s80C will be satisfied where the applicant has, or reasonably could have, made their claim in the safe third state.

29. Following a declaration of inadmissibility, the applicant's asylum claim will, for asylum support purposes, be treated as having been determined at the end of the 21-day period beginning with the day on which the secretary of state notifies the applicant of that decision. If the applicant is in receipt of IAA 1999 s95(1) support at this point, they will be notified that this support may end and that they may be able to apply for support under IAA 1999 s4(2).

Dependant

30. Regulation 2 of the AS Regulations 2000 defines a dependant as follows:

(4) In these Regulations "dependant", in relation to an asylum-seeker, a supported person or an applicant for asylum support, means, subject to paragraph (5), a person in the United Kingdom ("the relevant person") who—

(a) is his spouse;

(b) is a child of his or of his spouse, is dependant on him and is, or was at the relevant time, under 18;

(c) is a member of his or his spouse's close family and is, or was at the relevant time, under 18;

(d) had been living as part of his household—

(i) for at least six of the twelve months before the relevant time, or

(ii) since birth,

and is, or was at the relevant time, under 18;

(e) is in need of care and attention from him or a member of his household by reason of a disability and would fall within sub-paragraph (c) or (d) but for the fact that he is not, and was not at the relevant time, under 18;

(f) had been living with him as a member of an unmarried couple for at least two of the three years before the relevant time;

(g) is living as part of his household and was, immediately before 6th December 1999 (the date when the interim Regulations came into force), receiving assistance from a local authority under section 17 of the Children Act 1989(2);

(h) is living as part of his household and was, immediately before the coming into force of these Regulations, receiving assistance from a local authority under—

(i) section 22 of the Children (Scotland) Act 1995(3); or

(ii) Article 18 of the Children (Northern Ireland) Order 1995(4); or

(i) has made a claim for leave to enter or remain in the United Kingdom, or for variation of any such leave, which is being considered on the basis that he is dependant on the asylum-seeker;

31. Ultimately, these provisions mean that where an application for support is made by a dependant of the asylum seeker, it follows that the asylum seeker will be treated as a dependant of the applicant, so that they can be considered when assessing eligibility for support.

Destitution

32. Section 95(3) of the IAA 1999 outlines the relevant test for destitution. It provides that a person is destitute if:

- they do not have adequate accommodation or any means of obtaining it (whether or not their other essential living needs are met) or

- have adequate accommodation or the means of obtaining it but cannot meet their other essential living needs

33. Regulation 7 of the AS Regulations 2000 outlines the period within which the applicant must be likely to become destitute. Where the question of whether a person is destitute or likely to become so destitute falls to be determined in relation to an application for

asylum support, the relevant period is 14 days beginning with the day on which that question falls to be determined[12]. Where the question of destitution falls to be determined in relation to a supported person, the relevant period is 56 days beginning with the day on which that question falls to be determined[13].

34. Regulation 5 of the AS Regulations 2000 provides that where an application for asylum support has been made by an Applicant and one or more dependants, when considering the question of destitution, the Secretary of State must decide whether the Applicant and all those dependants, taken together, are destitute or likely to become destitute within the relevant period prescribed by regulation 7 (see above)[14].

35. Regulation 6 of the AS Regulations 2000 outlines the income and assets to be taken into account by the Secretary of State when determining the issue of destitution. The following must be ignored by the Secretary of State[15]:

- Any asylum support and any support under section 98 of the IAA 1999, which the applicant for asylum support or any dependant of his is provided with.

- In the scenario where the question is whether destitution is likely within a particular period, the Secretary of State must ignore any asylum support and any support under section 98 of the IAA 1999, which might be provided within that period.

---

12 AS Regulations 2000, Regulation 7(a)

13 AS Regulations 2000, Regulation 7(b)

14 AS Regulations 2000, Regulation 5

15 AS Regulations 2000, Regulation 6(3)

36. The following must be taken into account by the Secretary of State[16]:

- any other income which the principal, or any dependant of his, has or might reasonably be expected to have in that period;
- any other support which is available to the principal or any dependant of his, or might reasonably be expected to be so available in that period; and
- any assets mentioned in regulation 6(5) (whether held in the United Kingdom or elsewhere) which are available to the principal or any dependant of his otherwise than by way of asylum support or support under section 98, or might reasonably be expected to be so available in that period.

37. The assets mentioned in regulation 6(5) which the Secretary of State must take into account are:

(a) cash;

(b) savings;

(c) investments;

(d) land;

(e) cars or other vehicles; and

(f) goods held for the purpose of a trade or other business.

---

16 AS Regulations 2000, Regulation 6(4)

38. Any assets not mentioned above must be ignored by the Secretary of State. The 'Assessing Destitution' policy provides guidance on the typical types of income and assets that are covered by Regulation 6, and those which should be disregarded. For instance, in relation to bank accounts, the guidance states that:

> *"if it is established that a person seeking support has savings or funds held in a current, deposit, or some other account, evidence in the form of account books or statements is usually required to show the balance – it will usually be necessary to look at bank statements for the previous 6 months"*. [17]

39. With all of the above requirements and guidance in mind, we will now turn specifically to address the test for destitution.

Adequate accommodation

40. As noted above, a person is destitute if 'they do not have adequate accommodation or any means of obtaining it'. It is noteworthy that despite the reference to adequate accommodation, there is no definition for 'adequate' in the IAA 1999. As noted by Fordham J in *SA v SSHD* [2023]:

> *7. The legislation uses the idea of accommodation being "adequate" at two distinct stages (A §52). The first stage asks whether there is an absence of "adequate" existing accommodation, in testing whether there is destitution (s.95(3)(a), (5), (6)). The second stage requires the provision of "adequate" accommodation as the response to destitution*

[17] Assessing Destitution (version 3, 23 August 2023)

(s.96(1)(a)). The word "adequate" means the same thing at both stages. But the context is important (A §52).[18]

41. For the purposes of discussing eligibility, we are concerned with what Fordham J describes as the first stage.

42. When assessing whether a person and/or his dependants have adequate accommodation or any means of obtaining it, the Secretary of State must have regard to the following matters[19]:

(a) whether it would be reasonable for the person to continue to occupy the accommodation;

(b) whether the accommodation is affordable for him;

(c) whether the accommodation is provided under section 98 of the Act, or otherwise on an emergency basis, only while the claim for asylum support is being determined;

(d) whether the person can secure entry to the accommodation;

(e) where the accommodation consists of a moveable structure, vehicle or vessel designed or adapted for human habitation, whether there is a place where the person is entitled or permitted both to place it and reside in it;

(f) whether the accommodation is available for occupation by the person's dependants together with him;

(g) whether it is probable that the person's continued occupation of the accommodation will lead to domestic violence against him or any of his dependants.

---

18 *SA v SSHD* [2023] EWHC 1787

19 AS Regulations 2000, Regulation 8(3)

43. Furthermore, it is provided that "in determining whether it would be reasonable for a person to continue to occupy accommodation, regard may be had to the general circumstances prevailing in relation to housing in the district of the local housing authority where the accommodation is".[20]

44. In relation to "whether accommodation is affordable for him", the Secretary of State must have regard to the following:

> *(a) any income, or any assets mentioned in regulation 6(5) (whether held in the United Kingdom or elsewhere), which is or are available to him or any dependant of his otherwise than by way of asylum support or support under section 98 of the Act, or might reasonably be expected to be so available;*
>
> *(b) the costs in respect of the accommodation; and*
>
> *(c) the person's other reasonable living expenses.*

45. Section 95(5)(b) and (6) outline matters which the Secretary of State must not have regard to when assessing adequacy:

- the fact that the applicant concerned has no enforceable right to occupy the accommodation;
- the fact that the applicant shares the accommodation, or any part of the accommodation, with one or more other persons;
- the fact that the accommodation is temporary;
- he location of the accommodation.

---

20 AS Regulations 2000, Regulation 8(4)

It is common that an applicant will be living with friends or relatives at the time they apply for s95(1) support. The *Assessing destitution policy* indicates that they will normally be required to explain why this accommodation is no longer available.[21]

Essential living needs

46. As noted above, a person is destitute if 'they have adequate accommodation or the means of obtaining it but cannot meet their other essential living needs".

47. Regulation 9(4) of the AS Regulations 2000 outlines a list of items and expenses that cannot be treated as being an essential living need of a person for the purposes of determining destitution. These items and expenses are as follows:

    (a) the cost of faxes;

    (b) computers and the cost of computer facilities;

    (c) the cost of photocopying;

    (d) travel expenses, except the expense mentioned in paragraph (5);

    (e) toys and other recreational items;

    (f) entertainment expenses.

48. In deciding whether an item or expense can be considered as an essential living need, the starting point of this exercise must be the requirement in the Reception Directive for "full respect for human dignity, so as to ensure a dignified standard of living". In the case of

[21] Assessing Destitution (version 3, 23 August 2023), page 11

(Refugee Action) v SSHD, it was held that the following items could be considered as as essential living needs:

- *essential household goods such as washing powder, cleaning materials and disinfectant;*

- *nappies, formula milk and other special requirements of new mothers, babies and very young children;*

- *non-prescription medication;*

- *the opportunity to maintain interpersonal relationships and a minimum level of participation in social, cultural and religious life."*

How is s.95(1) support provided?

49. Section 96 IAA 1999 outlines the ways in which support may be provided under s95(1). Support may be provided as follows:

    (a) by providing accommodation appearing to the Secretary of State to be adequate for the needs of the supported person and his dependants (if any);

    (b) by providing what appear to the Secretary of State to be essential living needs of the supported person and his dependants (if any);

    (c) to enable the supported person (if he is the asylum-seeker) to meet what appear to the Secretary of State to be expenses (other than legal expenses or other expenses of a prescribed description) incurred in connection with his claim for asylum;

(d) to enable the asylum-seeker and his dependants to attend bail proceedings in connection with his detention under any provision of the Immigration Acts; or

(e) to enable the asylum-seeker and his dependants to attend bail proceedings in connection with the detention of a dependant of his under any such provision.

Relevant policies and guidance

50. The provision of asylum support is an area dealt with extensively in guidance issued by the SSHD. The SSHD has issued the Allocation of Asylum Accommodation Policy ('the Allocation Policy'), which provides relevant guidance on the allocation of asylum support:

a) "The overriding principle when allocating accommodation is that it is offered on a 'no choice basis".

b) "In considering requests to be allocated accommodation in a specific location, you must consider whether there are exceptional circumstances that make it appropriate to agree to the request. Exceptional circumstances should be considered on a case-by-case basis but may include, for example, serious risks around health and safety or security" (page 6).

c) "Evidence needed to support the request for accommodation in a particular location: Requests for accommodation in a particular location should normally be made in writing and be supported, where appropriate, with documentary evidence, for example from medical practitioners or professional experts. The reasons for the request should normally be fully supported by evidence of why accommodation in a particular location is necessary" (page 7).

d) "Medical treatment: You may receive requests to provide accommodation in a particular location because the individual is receiving medical treatment in that area. Care and treatment for most medical conditions is available in all parts of the UK and the transfer of responsibility for managing an individual's care and/or providing that treatment to different NHS organisations (or Health and Social care trusts in Northern Ireland) is a normal everyday occurrence within the NHS. Unless there are exceptional circumstances, requests to be provided with accommodation in a specific location solely on the grounds that medical care or treatment is already being provided in the area should therefore be refused, particularly if primary care based" (page 9).

e) For cases where the individual is pregnant you should consider the guidance set out in Healthcare needs and pregnancy dispersal (page 9).

51. One of the main areas of litigation in asylum support relates to the provision of support to vulnerable individuals, such as pregnant women. The SSHD has issued relevant guidance to Home Office staff responsible for dispersing asylum seekers/failed asylum seekers and their dependants who have health needs. This policy is known as the *Healthcare Needs and Pregnancy Dispersal Policy* (version 3.0. January 2016), and states as follows:

"***3.6 Initial Accommodation Team***

If an applicant is identified as receiving treatment for a severe or complex health need and the details of the treating clinician(s)/midwife are known, the IA Team should send a Treating Clinician Notification of Arrival in Initial Accommodation Letter to the treating clinician(s)/midwife as soon as possible after the applicant has been routed to his allocated IA

3.7. Initial Accommodation site health check

... During the IA health check the applicant may be identified as either receiving medical treatment or having healthcare needs, including pregnancy, which might have an impact on dispersal arrangements in the event the applicant is granted support under section 95. If this is the case, the IA Healthcare Team should provide the IA Team with adequate information to enable appropriate dispersal arrangements to be made at the earliest opportunity.

4.4 Role of the Asylum Support Medical Advisor

The Asylum Support Medical Adviser's role in the dispersal process, based upon the written medical evidence/reports submitted, is to:

- *Advise Home Office caseworkers about the general availability and capacity of medical treatment in particular regions;*

- *Advise on fitness to travel to dispersal accommodation;*

- *Recommend the nature of any accommodation to be provided;*

- *Advise on requirement to stay in a particular area for medical reasons;*

- *Advise on medical need to relocate supported persons/applicants from one area to another;*

4.6 Considering Medical Evidence

Applicants may submit medical evidence that may have an impact on the dispersal location or the nature of the property allocated. If caseworkers are unsure about what dispersal arrangements would be suitable as a result of the applicant's medical condition/treatment, advice may be requested from the Asylum Support Medical Adviser using the "Asylum Support Medical Adviser Referral Form".

Caseworkers must consider the advice of the Asylum Support Medical Adviser, but should also weigh the circumstances of each case against the relevant legislation and policy instructions. In the majority of cases, the caseworker should be able make a final decision on the applicant's dispersal requirements which balances the advice from the Asylum Support Medical Adviser on medical needs with access to appropriate housing.

4.9 Determining the nature of accommodation required

Where medical needs are identified, caseworkers should assess if and how these impact on the nature of accommodation required. As a general rule, where the Home Office is providing support, the following types of accommodation should normally be requested for the following groups: • Pregnant women: any dispersal property must be suitable not just for a pregnant woman (including mobility issues), but for a mother and baby, post birth;

… If it becomes evident that an applicant may have a care need which requires some additional help over and above provision of accommodation, caseworkers should liaise with the Local Authority to arrange a Communicate Care Assessment to determine whether support is required…

4.10 Location of accommodation

When determining locations of dispersal accommodation, decisions must be taken in adherence of the dispersal policy set out in the policy document – Dispersal: accommodation requests. Caseworkers must have regard to the desirability, in general, of providing accommodation in areas in which there is a ready supply of accommodation. This means that, as a general rule, unless there are circumstances which warrant dispersal to the London and the South East, caseworkers should allocate accommodation in areas outside London and the South East region. Accommodation is provided on a no-choice basis.

4.13 Requests from applicants to delay dispersal on grounds of ill health

From time to time, once arrangements for dispersal to asylum support accommodation have been made, representations are received from an applicant to either delay travel or amend dispersal arrangements on healthcare grounds. In such cases, caseworkers should take into consideration the written medical evidence supplied when determining whether to change the original dispersal date or location. In the majority of cases, if the information is received via a telephone call, the decision to change the original dispersal date or location should not be made until written medical evidence has been received. The Home Office retains the discretion to re-book or to take "failure to travel" action where the illness is minor, e.g. failing to travel due to having a cold or a skin rash. Caseworkers should bear in mind that some applicants may have difficulty in gauging the severity of a medical condition.

7.4 Pregnancy / New Mothers – Dispersal Guidelines

Pregnancy, birth and new motherhood have a significant impact on a woman's physical and psychological health, but the nature of that impact varies considerably between individuals. No single solution is likely to be in the interests of all pregnant women and each case should be sympathetically considered on its own merits and solutions sought in consultation with the woman.

Every effort should be made to protect the health of pregnant women, new mothers and their babies. Caseworkers who are responsible for dispersing pregnant applicants should seek to minimise stress to the woman during her pregnancy.

7.4.1 Risks during pregnancy

In September 2010, the National Institute for Health and Clinical Excellence (NICE) published a guideline that identified particular groups of pregnant women who are affected by complex social factors. One of the groups identified included women who are "recent migrants, asylum seekers, refugees or who have difficulty speaking or reading English".

The guideline makes clear that pregnant asylum

seeking women may be affected not only by complex social factors within the UK (lack of knowledge of the health system; problems with interpretation), but also by poor health and other medical concerns arising as a result of pre-arrival issues, such as:

- A poor overall health status;
- Underlying and possibly unrecognised medical conditions;

• Possible FGM issues;

• psychological and medical effects of flight from war torn countries;

• Fears about immigration; and

• Languages difficulties.

It is also recognised that maternal stress in pregnancy has a detrimental effect on subsequent childhood development.

Maternity care covers the entire period of pregnancy, labour, and the postnatal period. NICE has identified several key issues throughout this to improve pregnancy outcomes and safeguard

the health of mothers and babies. These are:

• Early booking into maternity services, ideally by 10 weeks gestation:

• Continuity of care;

• Family and social support;

• Planning labour;

• Post natal care for 6-8 weeks.

Given the potential for increased risks to the health of some women in these circumstances, caseworkers should try to avoid dispersing women away from the area in which they are living and receiving maternity care, and in which they can access social and family support. If dispersal is unavoidable, caseworker should take particular care when arranging accommodation for pregnant women and their children.

7.4.2 General background information on pregnancy

Asylum seekers/failed asylum seekers have an increased risk of mortality during pregnancy or soon afterwards compared with the indigenous population, and two of the key risk factors are late enrolment in maternity care or missed appointments.

Various tests are required at the first ante-natal visit and at specific intervals during pregnancy, including blood tests, an optional HIV test and ultrasound scans. Regular visits to a clinic ensure that blood pressure and other factors are within normal limits. Certain tests are relevant to the various stages of pregnancy and cannot be delayed. Caseworkers should therefore take care that dispersal does not disrupt this programme and particular care should be taken not to disrupt any anomaly screening which has been scheduled.

Following a birth, mother and baby are visited frequently by a midwife until day 14 (sometimes up to day 28) and then by a health visitor. This is followed by a post natal examination at 6 weeks.

Consideration may need to be given in both dispersal and IA to the number of flights of stairs women who have recently given birth need to negotiate in the short-term. More than one flight of stairs can be exhausting and painful.

Within the constraints of a no choice dispersal policy, it is likely that women will have individual preferences regarding the timing of their dispersal from IA. However, the aim, wherever possible, will be to settle them into accommodation where they will be able to access services throughout their pregnancy and into new motherhood, by:

A. *if possible, accommodating pregnant women as close to the maternity unit where they are currently accessing care, as well as existing sources of family and social support; or,*

B. *where there is no previous link to maternity services, disperse them from IA as soon as possible so that they can establish health and community links in the dispersal area and avoid disruption around delivery.*

No single solution is likely to be in the interests of all pregnant women and each case should be sympathetically considered on its own merits. […]

7.4.3 The Late Stages of Pregnancy

Caseworkers should be aware that many asylum seeking women have shorter pregnancies than the indigenous population and may well give birth earlier than the estimated date of delivery (EDD). Although the whole of pregnancy, labour and the postnatal period must be taken into account when considering dispersal, there are additional risks to women whose pregnancies have reached the late stages.

For the purposes of this policy, the late stages of pregnancy will be defined as normally running from six weeks before the Estimated Date of Delivery (EDD) until a clinician has signed off on the postnatal checks. The latter will usually be around six weeks after birth, unless there have been complications.

7.4.5 Dispersing asylum seeking women who are pregnant on arrival in the UK

Pregnant asylum seeking women who have recently arrived in the UK are unlikely to be registered with maternity services. As a result, it should be possible to disperse the women from Initial Accommodation (IA) to suitable accommodation as soon as possible.

If an applicant is in the late stages of pregnancy, as defined above, priority should be given to finding appropriate dispersal accommodation nearby so that she can continue to access the local maternity unit. If accommodation is not available within the area where the woman has booked into maternity services, then the options of either dispersal to another location or the deferral of dispersal should be considered in consultation with the applicant.

Dispersal in the late stages of pregnancy should only be undertaken either at the request of applicant or her treating medical practitioners. If such a request is made, it must be made in writing. Caseworkers should liaise with the IA Healthcare Team when making dispersal arrangements, taking advice from the independent Asylum Support Medical Adviser where appropriate.

Wherever possible, pregnant women should only be dispersed once whilst they are pregnant, unless they specifically request relocation. This means that any dispersal accommodation must be suitable to the woman's needs both before and after birth and available throughout that period.

There should be a dispersal notice period of at least ten calendar days between a pregnant woman in the late stages of pregnancy (as defined above) being advised of the area of her dispersal accommodation and her actual dispersal. The IA healthcare team should be notified of the intended dispersal, including the destination and the intended dispersal date, at the same time as the pregnant woman.

When making dispersal arrangements for such cases, caseworkers should liaise closely with the IA Healthcare Team to ensure that all issues relating to the set up and/or effective handover of of care, including any referrals to maternity services etc at the dispersal destination are completed before the dispersal takes place.

7.4.6 Dispersing pregnant asylum seeking women who have been residing in the UK for some time

When dispersing a pregnant woman who is already registered with maternity services, caseworkers should try to ensure that she is able to continue to live in her usual residential area. This would enable her to maintain access to her current maternity service and any other health and support services she may need access to, as well as maintaining any social support networks she has.

Wherever possible, pregnant women should only be dispersed once whilst they are pregnant, unless they specifically request relocation. This means that any dispersal accommodation must be suitable to the woman's needs both before and after birth and available throughout that period.

However, for those applying for support under section 95, it may prove necessary for them to spend some time in the nearest IA if they are unable to remain in their current private accommodation until appropriate dispersal accommodation is found. Every effort should be made to find appropriate accommodation in the area where the local maternity unit with which they are registered is located.

Whilst access to IA is generally not available to persons applying for support under section 4, if a woman is in the late stages of pregnancy (as defined above) and is either street homeless or imminently street homeless, consideration may be given to placing her in IA. This would enable access to the IA healthcare team for an assessment of fitness to travel and/or for dispersal, as well as providing assistance on either continuity of maternity and other care, or registration with maternity services, locally or at the dispersal destination.

If accommodation is not available within the area where the woman is registered with maternity services, as a last resort the options of either dispersal to another location or the deferral of dispersal should be considered in consultation with the applicant.

Dispersal in the late stages of pregnancy should only be undertaken either at the request of applicant or her treating medical practitioners. If such a request is made, it must be made in writing.

When making dispersal arrangements for such cases, caseworkers should liaise closely with the IA Healthcare Team to ensure that all issues relating to the set up and/or effective handover of care, including any referrals to maternity services etc at the dispersal destination are completed before the dispersal takes place.

Full use should be made of the dispersal notice period to ensure that where dispersal requires any travel, it should not take place before the views of either the IA health team or midwife/treating clinician on the following issues have been obtained:

The woman's fitness to travel;

- *any travel constraints (length of journey etc); and*

- *any arrival issues, including any arrangements that have been made, or need to be made, and with whom, to ensure effective handover of care.*

7.4.8 Other high risk pregnancies

Other high risk pregnancies include cases where a woman has a chronic disease or pregnancy related disorder such as pre-eclampsia. If accommodation is available, dispersal should occur to an area where they can reasonably be expected to access their current treating facility.

Section 98(1) support of the Immigration and Asylum Act 1999

Who is eligible for s98(1) support?

52. Support under s98(1) is effectively known as 'temporary support'. The provision of support under s98(1) ensures that while an applicant is waiting for the outcome of their application for s95(1) support, they can receive support in that interim period. Specifically, the Secretary of State is permitted to provide temporary support to:

    (a) asylum-seekers or dependants of asylum-seekers;

    (b) who it appears to the secretary of state may be destitute.

53. As outlined by s98(2), support may be provided under this section only until the Secretary of State is able to determine whether support may be provided under section 95.

54. As s98(2) falls under the same legal framework as s95(1), the following terms have the same meaning as explained earlier: 'asylum-seeker', 'dependant' and 'destitute'. The

55. Any challenge to a refusal to provide s98(1) support lies in a claim for judicial review.

56. The Home Office policy "Asylum support: policy bulletins instruction", provides the necessary details on the provision of support. The policy indicates that "it is temporary full board or self catering accommodation and is intended for short term use (full board former and operating hotels, houses in multiple occupation, hostels and self – contained self – catering properties)".

57. In relation to ending provision of initial accommodation under section 98, the policy states that "If a decision is taken not to provide S95 support, or because of Section 55 exclusion, initial accommodation to those supported under Section 98 must end as soon as is reasonable; ordinarily the next working day. Exceptionally this may be extended to 7 working days, but no longer. Exactly when Initial accommodation ends will depend on the individual case, for instance

CHAPTER TWO

SECTION 4(2) SUPPORT OF THE IMMIGRATION AND ASYLUM ACT 1999

1. In the previous chapter, we addressed the support available to asylum-seekers in the United Kingdom. In this chapter, we will look at the support available to failed asylum-seekers and their dependants under s4(2) of the Immigration and Asylum Act 1999.

Who is eligible for s4(2) support?

2. Under s4(2) IAA 1999 the Secretary of State may provide, or arrange for the provision of, facilities for the accommodation of a person if[22]:

    - He was (but is no longer) an asylum-seeker; and
    - His claim for asylum was rejected; or
    - His claim for asylum was declared inadmissible.

3. Under s4(3) IAA 1999 there is also a power to provide, or arrange for the provision of, facilities for the accommodation of a dependant of a person form whom facilities may be provided under s4(2) IAA 1999[23].

---

22 s4(2) IAA 1999

23 s4(3) IAA 1999

4. In addition to the abovementioned legislative provisions, there are also regulatory provisions which are relevant to this form of support. First, the Immigration and Asylum (Provision of Accommodation to Failed Asylum-Seekers) Regulations ('PAFAS Regs') 2005. This provides the eligibility criteria for support under s4(2) IAA 1999. Also, the Immigration and Asylum (Provision of Services or Facilities) Regulations ('PSF Regs') 2007. This outlines the nature of support provided under s4(2).

5. An applicant qualifies for support under s4(2) and 4(3) IAA 1999 if they satisfy the following criteria:

    a. they appear to the secretary of state to be destitute[24]; and moreover

    b. they satisfy one or more of the following criteria, prescribed under the PAFAS Regs 2005[25]:

        (i) He is taking all reasonable steps to leave the UK or place themself in a position in which he is able to leave the UK, which may include complying with attempts to obtain a travel document to facilitate their departure.[26]

        (ii) He is unable to leave the UK by reason of a physical impediment to travel or for some other medical reason.[27]

24 PAFAS Regs 2005 reg 3(1)(a)

25 PAFAS Regs 2005 reg 3(1)(b)

26 PAFAS Regs 2005 reg 3(2)(a)

27 PAFAS Regs 2005 reg 3(2)(b)

(iii) He is unable to leave the UK because in the opinion of the secretary of state there is currently no viable route of return available.[28]

(iv) He has made an application for judicial review of a decision in relation to his asylum claim and has been granted permission to proceed by the court.[29]

(v) The provision of accommodation is necessary for the purpose of avoiding a breach of a person's ECHR rights, within the meaning of the Human Rights Act 1998.[30]

6. Failed asylum-seekers must additionally establish that they meet one or more of the five conditions above in reg 3(1) of the PAFAS Regs.

7. We will now turn to look at the specific terms which are relevant to understanding s4(2) support.

Was, but is no longer, an asylum-seeker

8. The definition of asylum seeker is a person[31]:

- who is not under 18;
- who has made a claim for asylum;
- which has been recorded by the secretary of state;

---

28 PAFAS Regs 2005 reg 3(2)(c)

29 PAFAS Regs 2005 reg 3(2)(d)

30 PAFAS Regs 2005 reg 3(2)(e)

31 s4(4) IAA 1999

- which has not been determined.

Has had their claim for asylum rejected

9. A claim will be deemed rejected following a decision by the Secretary of State to refuse an asylum claim on the basis that the Applicant does not satisfy the requirements for refugee status. It is also necessary that the Applicant is appeal rights exhausted.

Has had their claim for asylum declared inadmissible

10. There are certain circumstances in which the Secretary of State must declare an asylum claim to be inadmissible. In circumstances where an applicant is a national of an EU member state, the claim must be declared inadmissible.

Destitution

11. What does destitute mean? For the purposes of s4(2), an Applicant satisfies the requirements for destitution if they[32]:

    (a) do not have adequate accommodation or any means of obtaining it (whether or not their other essential living needs are met); or

    (b) have adequate accommodation or the means of obtaining it, but cannot meet their other essential living needs.

12. In short, this is by and large the same definition which exists under s95. The point of divergence between s4(2) and s95(1) is that under

32 s95(3) IAA 1999

s4(2), an applicant will only qualify if they appear to be destitute now (as opposed to in 14 days).

13. However, as outlined in the section 4(2) policy, the position is that a 14-day period applies to section 4(2) support applicants. Where an applicant is already receiving support, it is a 56-day period.

Five conditions to receive s4(2) support

14. Section 4(2) of the IA 1999 states that the applicant must qualify under one or more of the following conditions outlined in reg 3(2) of the PAFAS Regs.

Reg 3(2)(a) Taking all reasonable steps to leave the UK

15. To satisfy this condition, applicants are required to demonstrate that they are taking 'all reasonable steps' to leave the UK or to place themselves in a position in which they are able to leave the UK.

16. There is no statutory definition for what reasonable step means.

17. The s4(2) policy states that eligibility under this condition should be 'reviewed regularly and should usually be discontinued after 3 months unless the person provides satisfactory evidence to show why they have not left the UK[33].

18. The s4(2) policy outlines factors to be taken into account in determining whether an applicant is taking all reasonable steps[34]. In particular, consideration should be given to whether the applicant:

---

33 The Section 4(2) policy, p9

34 The Section 4(2) policy, p10

(a) has applied for Assisted Voluntary Return (AVR);

(b) has applied to their national embassy for any necessary travel document needed to facilitate their departure from the UK;

(c) has fully complied with the Home Office's processes to obtain a travel document on their behalf, including by supplying accurate information to support an application for an Emergency Travel Document;

(d) is being prosecuted under Asylum and Immigration (Treatment of Applicants, etc) Act 2004 s35 because they have failed to comply with directions issued by the secretary of state to take specified action to assist with the re-documentation process.

Reg 3(2)(b) – Unable to leave the UK

19. Under this condition, applicants must show that they are 'unable to leave the United Kingdom by reason of a physical impediment to travel or for some other medical reason'. What must be demonstrated is that the applicant has a physical or medical condition which means that they are 'unable' to travel 'on any given day'[35].

20. In *R (SSHD) v Chief Asylum Support Adjudicator, Osman and others,* Holman J outlined the following approach to considering this condition:

(a) It is necessary to consider whether the applicant is unable to leave the UK;

---

[35] R (SSHD) v Chief Asylum Support Adjudicator, Osman and others [2006] EWHC 1248 (Admin) at para 60 per Holman J

(b) If so, it is then necessary to determine whether that inability to leave is by reason of a physical impediment to travel or some other medical reason.[36]

21. Osman J observed that the word 'unable' meant the same thing as 'not able', as opposed to 'impossible'.

Pregnancy and maternity

22. The s4(2) policy states as follows with regard to pregnant women:

> *Unless there are complications with the pregnancy, supported by medical evidence that the person's health and or that of the unborn child may be at risk, support must not normally be granted until around 6 weeks before the EDD [expected delivery date].*[37]

Psychological and mental health conditions

23. This condition can also be satisfied if the Applicant is unable to travel because of another 'medical reason'. There is no statutory definition of what 'medical reason' means.

Medical evidence

24. It will be incumbent on the Applicant to provide medical evidence from a medical practitioner regarding the nature of the physical

---

[36] [2006] EWHC 1248 (Admin) at para 21 per Holman J.

[37] The Section 4(2) policy, p11

impediment or medical reason that prevents the person from leaving the UK.

Reg 3(2)(c) – No viable route of return

25. Under this condition, the Secretary of State may provide support where the applicant is unable to leave the UK because, there is currently no viable route of return available.

Reg 3(2)(d) Permission granted in judicial review

26. Under this condition, an applicant will be eligible for support where they have made an application for judicial review in England or Wales in relation to their asylum claim and have been granted permission to proceed to a substantive hearing. It is important to note that this condition is limited to judicial review challenges relating to the applicant's asylum claim.

27. It is for the Applicant to demonstrate the existence of a judicial review claim and the grant of permission.

Reg 3(2)(e) Support to avoid a breach of human rights

28. An applicant under this condition must establish that the provision of accommodation is necessary for the purpose of avoiding a breach of a person's 'Convention rights' within the meaning of the Human Rights Act 1998.

29. Differently to the other conditions, reg 3(2)(e) does not focus solely on the applicant. It is concerned with whether the Applicant needs accommodation in order to avoid a breach of 'a person's' rights under the ECHR – this could mean a dependant.

30. In *R (SSHD) v First-tier Tribunal (Social Entitlement Chamber)*, Chamberlain J stated that it would 'not be wise, to attempt to define here the precise boundaries of the category of destitute failed asylum-seekers whose ECHR rights require the provision of accommodation under reg 3(2)(e)' and 'a multifactorial assessment would be required in each individual case'[38].

31. In R (Clue) v Birmingham City Council [2010] EWCA Civ 460, Dyson LJ outlined the following approach[39]:

   (a) It is necessary to decide whether and, if so, the extent to which it is necessary to exercise a power or perform a duty for the purpose of avoiding a breach of a person's rights under the ECHR. If the withholding of assistance would not cause a person to suffer from destitution amounting to a breach of their rights under the ECHR (typically Article 3), the investigation ends there.

   (b) However, if there are no other sources of assistance which would save the person from destitution amounting to a breach of a right under the ECHR, it is necessary consider whether there is a practical or legal impediment to the person returning to their country of origin. If, and only if, such an impediment exists, then support will need to be provided.

32. This approach has been adopted in the Section 4(2) policy.

---

38 "R (SSHD) v First-tier Tribunal (Social Entitlement Chamber) [2021] EWHC 1690 (Admin) at para 137 per Chamberlain J."

39 "R (Clue) v Birmingham City Council [2010] EWCA Civ 460, [2011] 1 WLR 99 at paras 53–75."

33. In *R (Limbuela)* v SSHD, Lord Bingham explained that:[40]

> *A general public duty to house the homeless or provide for the destitute cannot be spelled out of article 3. But I have no doubt that the threshold may be crossed if a late applicant with no means and no alternative sources of support, unable to support himself, is, by the deliberate action of the state, denied shelter, food or the most basic necessities of life.*

34. Lord Bingham went on to state that the relevant Article 3 threshold would be crossed '*if there were persuasive evidence that a late applicant was obliged to sleep in the street, save perhaps for a short and foreseeably finite period, or was seriously hungry, or unable to satisfy the most basic requirements of hygiene*'[41].

35. There is some commonality between the Article 3 ECHR threshold and the statutory destitution test contained in the IAA 1999. A failed asylum-seeker who is seeking support under s4(2) because they are facing imminent homelessness is likely to satisfy both the statutory destitution test for the purposes of ref 3(1) of PAFAS Regs 2005 and to meet the Article 3 threshold for the purposes of reg 3(2)(e).

36. There are scenarios similar to the case-law or guidance in which a destitute applicant may, or may arguably, face a practical or legal impediment to return such as to give rise to an entitlement to s4(2) support through this condition. These include cases:

    (a) in which further submissions have, or are to be, made;

---

[40] "R (Limbuela) v SSHD [2005] UKHL 66, [2006] 1 AC 396 at para 7 per Lord Bingham"

[41] "R (Limbuela) v SSHD [2005] UKHL 66, [2006] 1 AC 396 at para 9 per Lord Bingham"

(b) where the applicant has an extant application for leave to remain under ECHR Article 8 or other grounds;

(c) where the applicant has been referred to the National Referral Mechanism (NRM), the formal identification process for victims of trafficking, for a decision as to whether they are victims of trafficking;

(d) where the applicant is preparing to seek, or has applied for, judicial review of an asylum decision, but permission has not yet been granted;

(e) where the applicant is seeking to pursue an out of time appeal against the refusal of their asylum claim;

(f) where an applicant is pursuing an appeal against the rejection of an ECHR Article 3 claim having had his or her claim under the Refugee Convention declared inadmissible;

(g) where the applicant has made an application to the European Court of Human Rights (ECtHR);

(h) where the applicant needs to remain in the UK temporarily because of court proceedings,

37. The Section 4(2) policy reminds decision-makers that situations in which there is said to be an obstacle to return must be considered on a case-by-case basis. A few examples from this list are considered below.

Further submissions

38. It is common for applicants to make further submissions in support of a fresh claim for asylum under Immigration Rules para 353 – this will constitute an impediment. Para 353A of the Immigration Rules

prevents the Secretary of State removing an Applicant while further submissions are being considered.

39. The s4(2) policy provides that an applicant who has lodged further submissions, which have yet to be considered, who does not have access to accommodation and the means to live (or will shortly be in this position) may require support in order to avoid a breach of their rights under the ECHR[42].

40. Although the policy is couched in discretionary terms, support is provided in the majority of such cases, consistently with Immigration Rules para 353A, which provides that an applicant is not to be removed before the secretary of state has considered the further submissions under Immigration Rules para 353 or otherwise. However, support will be refused where the further submissions are found to be 'clearly abusive, manifestly unfounded or repetitious'.

Pre-permission judicial review claims

41. The case of *NS v First-tier Tribunal*[43] established that applicants who are seeking judicial review of an immigration decision, but have not yet been granted permission to proceed, may potentially face an impediment to return for the purposes of reg 3(2)(e). A number of specific instances in which the lodging of a judicial review claim will operate as an impediment to an applicant's removal from the UK may be found in the Home Office policy on Judicial reviews and injunctions. The policy provides that the threat of judicial review by itself does not require removal action to be deferred.

---

42 The Section 4(2) policy, p13

43 "R (NS (Somalia)) v First Tier Tribunal (Social Entitlement Chamber) [2009] EWHC 3819 (Admin)

Accommodation under s4(2)

42. As noted in the section 4(2) policy, those who receive the support are generally provided with accommodation and a payment card (the Aspen card) that can be used to buy food and other essential items.

43. With regard to the location of the accommodation, the policy provides that:

> *"Those granted support under section 4(2) are provided with accommodation on a no-choice basis, which will usually be outside London and the south-east of England. However, the caseworker may exceptionally consider providing accommodation in a particular location if there are particular reasons to do so, for example medical reasons*
>
> *The Asylum Support Medical Adviser is able to provide advice on:*
>
> • *the general availability of medical treatment in a particular region of the UK that the person may need to access*
>
> • *the person's fitness to travel to the region*
>
> • *any specific type of accommodation the person may need to be provided with because of a medical reason"*

Adequacy

44. There is no statutory requirement that accommodation provided to failed asylum-seekers under s4(2) is 'adequate' – this is different to the position under s95(1). However, it is arguable that as s4(2) accommodation is provided to those who are destitute and unable to obtain adequate accommodation other than by the provision of

statutory support that, read together with PAFAS Regs 2005 reg 3(1), there is an implicit, if not explicit, requirement for facilities provided to the applicant to be adequate. This statutory objective would be defeated by the provision of accommodation which is inadequate.

45. Applicants who find themselves housed in substandard conditions may seek to raise this with the Home Office or with their accommodation provider. The next step if these does not achieve the required results is to challenge the adequacy of accommodation by way of judicial review, depending on the nature of the inadequacy and the applicant's personal situation.

Subsistence

46. Subsistence payments are generally made at a standard rate of £45 per week, in line with s95(1) rates, which is intended to cover 'food, clothing and toiletries'. However, those in full-board accommodation, whose needs should be partially met by the provision of food at the accommodation, receive a weekly payment of only £8.392 In contrast with s95(1), there is no specified power in statute to set the level of financial support to be provided to failed asylum-seekers.

47. The weekly financial support rate is, instead, set by an exercise of the secretary of state's general power under s4(2).

48. To access their support, applicants are provided with an ASPEN payment card, to which these payments are loaded, which can be used at shops that accept Visa. However, unlike the ASPEN card which is provided to asylum-seekers in receipt of s95(1) support, the section 4(2) card cannot be used to withdraw cash from ATMs.

Travel

49. The secretary of state may supply, or arrange for the supply of, facilities for travel for a 'qualifying journey' for an applicant who is in receipt of support under s4(2), in order for them to:

    (a) receive healthcare treatment, where the applicant has provided evidence that the qualifying journey is necessary; or

    (b) register a birth.

50. In such cases, where necessary, arrangements can also be made for the applicant's dependants to travel too.

Conditions

51. The provision of support under s4(2) may be subject to conditions requiring the applicant or any dependant to[44]:

    (a) comply with specified standards of behaviour;

    (b) comply with a reporting requirement;

    (c) comply with a requirement to reside at an authorised address;

    (d) comply with a requirement to limit any absences from that address to no more than seven consecutive days and nights or no more than a total of 14 days and nights in any six-month period, unless the secretary of state grants permission to be away for longer than this;

    (e) comply with specified steps to facilitate their departure from the UK. Such conditions might include a requirement that

[44] "PAFAS Regs 2005 reg 6

the applicant applies for a passport from their national embassy or attends a Home Office re-documentation interview and provides accurate information to support an application for an Emergency Travel Document.

52. Any such conditions must be set out in writing, and will generally be provided with the decision letter granting the applicant support. Breach of any such conditions may lead to support being discontinued.

Applying for s4(2) support

53. S4(2) applications are made using form ASF1. This is the same form used to make s95(1) support applications.

54. The organisation, Migrant Help assists with applications and are ultimately the interface with the Home Office. Migrant Help assist applicants with completing applications and provide information on the process. Once the ASF1 is completed, the form is sent to the Home Office.

55. The s4(2) policy states that "If the information requested is not provided within 14 days, the application should be refused on the basis that the person has not established that they are eligible to receive support.

Dependants

56. Section 4(3) of the 1999 act enables the dependants of failed asylum seekers to be supported. As outlined in the policy: "Dependants include spouses, civil partners, people who have lived as husband and wife for 2 of the last 3 years, children and other close family members who have a disability. There is no requirement for the dependant to have been treated as a

dependant on the person's asylum claim"[45]. Applicants should indicate in the ASF1 that they are applying for support for themselves and dependants.

Time for decision-making

57. The Section 4(2) policy states as follows in relation to decision-making and how long this may take:

> *"... a decision on the application should not be unnecessarily delayed to await the further submissions decision. Generally, decisions should be made within 5 working days, but careful consideration should be given to any additional factors that call for the case to be given higher priority and the decision made more quickly.*
>
> *Where the following circumstances apply, reasonable efforts should be made to decide the application within 2 working days (the list is not exhaustive):*
>
> *(a) people who are street homeless;*
>
> *(b) families with minors;*
>
> *(c) disabled people;*
>
> *(d) elderly people;*
>
> *(e) pregnant women;*
>
> *(f) persons who have been subjected to torture, rape, or other serious forms of psychological, physical or sexual violence;*

[45] Immigration and Asylum Act 1999, Section 4(3)

(g) *potential victims of trafficking*".

Refusing or discontinuing support

58. The s4 policy states as follows in relation to refusing or discontinuing support:

> Where it is decided to refuse support or to stop providing it, a letter setting out the reasons must be sent to the person, copied to their representative if they have one. Where the decision is to stop providing support the person should be informed that the decision will take effect 14 working days from the date of the letter. The accommodation provider should also be given separate notice of the decision, with instructions that any eviction notice served on the person should ordinarily give them no less than 7 days to vacate the accommodation.

CHAPTER THREE

JUDICIAL REVIEW AND ASYLUM SUPPORT

What is judicial review

1. Judicial review provides a set of legal standards, enforced through a process of litigation, to enable people to challenge the lawfulness of decisions made by public bodies and others exercising public functions. In summary, judicial review provides a mechanism by which decisions, acts and failures of a public body can be challenged on the basis that it has acted unlawfully. Judicial review is a court process, and is primarily litigated in the Administrative Court – a specialist court within the High Court of Justice.

2. In judicial review proceedings, the main actors are: (1) the Claimant – challenging the decision taken by a public body, (2) the Defendant – the public body who has made that decision, (3) the Court – review the decision under challenge and assess whether it can be impugned on public law grounds, (4) Interested parties and Interveners.

3. To understand the judicial review process, there are numerous legal standards which outline public law principles that public bodies must adhere to. These are as follows[46]:

    a. Public bodies must have legal authority for their actions. This may be derived from statute, the common law or (in the case of some central government functions) a prerogative power. Public bodies must act within the scope of that legal authority.

[46] De Smith's Judicial Review, 9th Edition, page 256

b. Powers must be exercised within the objects and purpose of the statute.

c. Where a statute gives a public body discretionary power, that power must be used to further the scope and object of the statute—not for an extraneous purpose.

d. Public bodies must take into account all legally relevant considerations and avoid taking into account those that are irrelevant.

e. Where a statute gives decision-making power to a public body, that body (not another one) must exercise its discretion: except in some recognised circumstances, it is unlawful to delegate the power.

f. Fair procedures must be followed: these may be found in legislation, the common law and the Human Rights Act 1998. They may, according to the context, include requirements: to give notice of a proposed decision before making it; to consult and receive written representations; to disclose information before a final decision is reached; to provide oral hearings; and to give reasons for a decision.

g. Where a statute gives a public body discretionary power, the public body acts unlawfully if it adopts a rigid policy, with no exceptions, as to how the discretion will be exercised.

h. Public bodies act unlawfully if they are actually biased. They also act unlawfully if a fair-minded and informed observer, having considered the facts, would conclude that there was a real possibility of bias.

i. A public body's decision is unlawful if its substance is "unreasonable" or "irrational". This may involve: giving manifestly inappropriate weight to a factor; being illogical, arbitrary, inconsistent or uncertain: giving inadequate or incomprehensible reasons; or making a decision based on inadequate or mistaken facts.

j. A public body's decision is unlawful if it is disproportionate. One test of proportionality is to assess whether the action pursues a legitimate aim recognised by the law, whether the action is capable of achieving that aim, and whether a less restrictive alternative could have been employed. Generally, that kind of "structured proportionality" review is confined to the assessment of whether rights under the European Convention on Human Rights (ECHR) may be limited. However, proportionality can also engage when a decision-maker manifestly fails to attain a fair balance of (relevant) considerations, or where the impact of the decision is unduly oppressive.

k. Unless Parliament speaks clearly to the contrary in a statute, a decision-maker should act in compliance with the rule of law, including access to justice and the principle of equality.

l. A public body acts unlawfully if it creates a legitimate expectation (for example, by giving a clear and unambiguous assurance) that a particular procedure will be followed or a lawful benefit conferred from which it later seeks to resile without an adequate justification.

m. Under the Human Rights Act 1998 s.6 it is unlawful for a public body, or a person exercising functions of a public nature, to breach one of the rights of the ECHR (Convention rights) incorporated into national law.

4. Ultimately, it is for the court to adjudicate on whether a legal standard has been breached. The judicial review process commences with the Claimant seeking permission by the Administrative Court. If permission is granted, the matter moves on to a substantive hearing

before a judge. The judge will then provide a written judgment following a substantive hearing on whether the public body acted unlawfully.

Who has standing to bring a claim for judicial review?

5. In order to initiate a claim for judicial review, it is necessary for the relevant individual or organisation to have 'standing'. Under CPR Pt 54[47], this is expressed as the need for the claimant to have "sufficient interest". In relation to the ground of review that there is a breach of a Convention right, a further requirement that the claimant be a "victim" is imposed. In some other forms of public law proceedings, the term "person aggrieved" is used.

6. The courts have not provided a definition as to what sufficient interest means. But for our purposes, it will suffice that a person affected by a decision taken regarding asylum support (i.e. applicant or dependant of the applicant) will have standing to bring a claim for judicial review. There are also circumstances where groups and organisations will be deemed to have sufficient interest on certain issues.

What is under challenge in a judicial review?

7. Decisions, acts, and failures to act by public bodies exercising their public functions are all potentially challengeable by judicial review. Public bodies may be thought of as bodies that deliver a public service.

47 Civil Procedure Rules, Part 54

Public bodies 'exercise their public functions' when they carry out the work they were created for.

8. Some public functions are contracted out to private companies. If a private company is exercising a public function, its behaviour will be governed by public law principles, and its decisions, acts and failures to act are potentially challengeable by judicial review. For example, a private company that runs a prison is exercising a public function, and so its behaviour in treatment of prisoners is governed by public law.

What are the remedies?

9. When a Claimant brings a judicial review claim, it is necessary for the Claimant to seek relief(s). What is sought by the Claimant is known as remedies or orders. In judicial review claims, the following orders may be sought:

    a. A mandatory order – The nature of this order is that the court compels public authorities to fulfil their duties. For instance, the court may direct that the public body takes a new decision.

    b. A quashing order – This is an order which overturns or nullifies the decision being challenged, so that it has no legal effect. This is the most common outcome of successful judicial reviews. If the court makes a quashing order it can send the case back to the original decision maker directing it to remake the decision in light of the court's findings.

    c. A prohibiting order – This order prevents a tribunal or authority from acting beyond the scope of its powers. The key difference is that a prohibiting order acts prospectively by telling an authority not to do something in contemplation. In summary, it stops a public body from taking an unlawful decision or action that it has not yet taken.

d. A declaration – This is an order stating clearly and concisely what the law is, where this is disputed. This order clarifies the respective rights and obligations of the parties to the proceedings, without actually making any order. Unlike the remedies of quashing, prohibiting and mandatory order the court is not telling the parties to do anything in a declaratory judgment.

e. A declaration of incompatibility This is a special type of declaration that a particular provision of an Act of Parliament contravenes the Human Rights Act. It is not binding on Parliament, but is an invitation to MPs to change the law so that it complies the Human Rights Act.

f. Damages The court can order damages only if some other form of legal remedy is also being sought. There are limited circumstances in which damages may be ordered:

- where there is a right to damages under private law but you need to bring the judicial review proceedings to establish an element of the damages claim (for example, you need to show that a period of detention was unlawful, before you can claim compensation for it); or

- where there has been a breach of your human rights under the Human Rights Act 1998; or – where there has been a breach of your rights under European Union Law.

10. In addition, the court can grant an interim injunction. This is a temporary order requiring a public body to do something or not to do something until a final decision has been made in the case.

11. It is important to remember that the remedies outlined above are discretionary. Even if the court finds that a public body has acted wrongly it does not have to grant a remedy. It will make its decision

based on the circumstances and what it considers appropriate, fair and practical.

12. As can be seen from the list of remedies above, the court will not normally re-take the public body's decision itself, even if you win your judicial review. Instead, the court will normally order the public body to reconsider its decision, this time in accordance with the law that the court has now made clear. It may be possible in those circumstances for the public body to reach the same decision but this time by a lawful procedure. So it is possible that even if you win a judicial review, you may still not get what you want.

What are the grounds of JR?

Acting outside their powers

13. Public bodies are generally only free to do what the law says they can do.16 With some exceptions, the law is set out in Acts of Parliament and in secondary legislation (typically things like regulations, rules and orders) made by government ministers. So, with some exceptions, every decision a public body takes must be authorised by a piece of legislation, which will define any limits on the public body's powers.

14. Public bodies must correctly understand and apply the law that regulates and limits their decision-making powers. If they do not follow the law correctly any resulting decision, act, or failure to act will be unlawful

Use of Discretion by Public Authorities

15. As well as the limits placed on public bodies' powers in legislation, the judges have developed public law rules over many years that impose further restrictions on what public bodies can do. For

example, where the law gives a public body the 'discretion' to take a decision as it sees fit, public law regulates the public body's power in a number of ways, including by requiring it:

a. to take into account only relevant information and to disregard all irrelevant information;

b. to address the right question, and take reasonable steps to obtain the information necessary to make a properly informed decision; and,

c. to make sure they have not limited, or 'fettered', their discretion by applying a very rigid policy as if it were the law.

16. There may be relevant external guidance (for example guidance from government departments about how local authorities exercise certain powers), or a policy issued by the public body itself, to make sure that powers are used consistently and fairly in each case. Public bodies should take such guidance and policy into account when they exercise their legal powers. Guidance and policy are not law, and do not have to be followed, but they should be followed unless there is good reason not to. If a public body decides not to follow its own policy, or not to follow external guidance, it should normally give reasons.

Irrationality and proportionality

17. The courts may intervene to quash a decision where they consider it to be so demonstrably unreasonable as to be "irrational" or "perverse". The test is whether a decision "is so unreasonable that no reasonable authority could ever have come to it". In practice this is very difficult to show, and it is usually argued alongside other grounds.

18. In some cases, particularly where European law or human rights law regulates the public body's powers, a public body is required to act proportionately.

19. The concept of proportionality involves a balancing exercise between the legitimate aims of the state on one hand, and the protection of the individual's rights and interests on the other. The test is whether the means employed to achieve the aim correspond to the importance of the aim, and are no more intrusive on the rights of the individual affected than is necessary to achieve the aim. By way of example, to use a sledgehammer to crack a nut (when a nutcracker would do) would not be acting proportionately

Fairness of Procedure

20. A public body must never abuse its power by acting unfairly. If you are affected by a decision that a public body (including courts and tribunals) is going to take, you must be treated fairly. That means, among other things, that you are entitled to know the case against you if there is one, and have a proper opportunity to put your case.

21. A public body must be – and be seen to be – impartial, that is it must not give the appearance of being biased (whether or not it is actually biased). It must not allow decisions to be taken by people who have a financial interest in the outcome or a personal relationship with one of the parties that could give the appearance of bias.

22. If there are express procedures laid down by law that a public body must follow in order to reach a decision, then it must follow them. For example, a public body may be under a duty to consult people who it believes may be affected by a decision before the decision is made, perhaps because the law says there is such a duty, or perhaps because people have been consulted on similar proposals in the past.

and so have a reasonable expectation that they will be consulted again.

What is the procedure for applying for JR?

23. The procedure for applying for judicial review is outlined in CPR part 54. In addition to this there are accompanying practice directions. Beyond this, there is a comprehensive Administrative Court Judicial Review Guide, which provides a step-by-step guide to the judicial review process. This is a useful starting point.

Pre-action stage

24. Before any proceedings for judicial review are initiated, there are numerous practical steps which must be adhered to. Where a public body has taken a decision you think is unlawful, it is important to follow the Judicial Review Pre-action Protocol. It is very important to follow the Protocol before commencing a claim, for two reasons: first, it may serve to resolve the issue without need of litigation or at least to narrow the issues in the litigation; secondly, if the Protocol has not been followed the party or parties responsible may be subject to costs sanctions. Ultimately, litigation should be a last resort.

25. Stage one of the Protocol requires the parties to consider whether a method of alternative dispute resolution ("ADR") would be more appropriate. The Protocol mentions discussion and negotiation, referral to the Ombudsman and mediation (a form of facilitated negotiation assisted by an independent neutral party).

26. Stage two is to send the defendant a pre-action letter. The letter should be in the format outlined in Annex A to the Protocol. The letter should contain the date and details of the act or omission being challenged and a clear summary of the facts on which the claim is based. It should also contain details of any relevant information the

claimant is seeking and an explanation of why it is relevant. You should state your intention to apply for judicial review if they do not confirm they will take the action you have specified within a certain time, usually 14 days.

27. The defendant should normally be given 14 days to respond to the pre-action letter and must do so in the format outlined in Annex B to the Protocol. Where necessary, the defendant may ask for additional time to respond. The claimant should allow the defendant a reasonable time to respond, where that is possible in the circumstances of the case and without putting the time limits for starting the case in jeopardy

The permission stage

28. If there is no satisfactory response to the letter before claim, the next step is to make an application for permission to apply for judicial review. However, before the claim is initiated, there are numerous important issues to consider.

29. Time limits: Claims for judicial review must be started promptly and, in any event, not later than 3 months after the grounds for making the claim first arose. The primary requirement is to start the claim promptly. Even if the claim has been commenced within 3 months from the date of the conduct challenged, it may still be out of time if the claimant did not start the claim promptly.

30. The time limit may not be extended by agreement between the parties. However, it can be extended by the Court in its discretion and a prior agreement not to take a time point can be relevant to the exercise of that discretion. Where the claim challenges a decision, the time limit begins to run from the date the decision to be challenged was made (not the date when the claimant was informed about the decision).

31. All judicial review claims must be started by filing a Claim Form in the ACO. The date of filing, usually written on the Claim Form in manuscript by the ACO staff when the Claim Form is received at the ACO, is to be distinguished from the date of issue which is the date shown by the Court seal which is applied when the Claim Form is issued by the ACO. A claim for judicial review is made on the date on which it is filed.

32. The claimant is required to apply for permission to apply for judicial review in the Claim Form. When the Claim Form is filed, it must be accompanied by the relevant fee. If the relevant fee is not paid, the Claim Form will be returned unissued together with any accompanying documentation.

33. When the Claim Form is filed, certain particulars must be provided. These can be included in the Claim Form itself or on a separate document or documents accompanying it. The required particulars are:

    a. statement of the facts relied on, set out in numbered paras (in section 5 of the Claim Form or a separate document);

    b. a clear and concise statement of the grounds for bringing the claim, again set out in numbered paragraphs;

    c. where the claim includes a claim for damages under the Human Rights Act 1998, the claim for damages must be properly pleaded and particularised (in section 4 of the Claim Form or on a separate document);

    d. The statement of material facts and the statement of the grounds for bringing the claim can be included in a single document called a "Statement of Facts and Grounds. The statement of grounds should identify each ground of challenge; identify the relevant provision or principle of law said to have been breached; and concisely provide sufficient detail of the alleged breach to enable the parties and the Court to identify the essential issues. Each ground should raise a distinct issue in relation to the decision under challenge. Arguments and submissions in support of the grounds should be set out separately in relation to each ground.

34. The documentation must be provided in an indexed and paginated claim bundle. The papers are served on the public body, and on anyone (be they individuals, companies, or public bodies) who will be affected by the proceedings and may wish to participate.

35. Once the claim is issued by the court, you are known as 'the claimant' in the case and the public body as 'the defendant'. Others who have been served with the papers and wish to participate in the case are known as 'interested parties'.

36. Any defendant or interested party served with the Claim Form who wishes to take part in the permission stage of the judicial review claim must file and serve an Acknowledgment of Service.

37. The Acknowledgment of Service must be filed at the ACO within 21 days after service of the Claim Form. The 21-day period may be extended or shortened by judicial order. A judge may also consider permission to apply for judicial review without waiting for an Acknowledgment of Service to be filed.

38. The Acknowledgment of Service must set out the summary grounds for contesting the claim (or summary grounds of defence), the legal basis of the defendant's response to the claimant's case and any relevant facts (including any material matters of factual dispute), if the party does contest it. The summary grounds should provide a brief summary of the reasoning underlying the decision or conduct challenged, or reasons why the application for permission can be determined without that information. Ultimately, this is the opportunity for the Defendant to indicate why permission should not be granted.

39. The defendant public body and any interested parties usually have 21 days from when they receive the claim documents from you to file an acknowledgment of service and set out grounds if they are going to argue that the claim is unarguable, and should not be granted permission to proceed.

40. All of the papers are put before a judge who decides whether to grant permission to proceed to a full hearing. The judge can make the following orders:

    a. to grant permission to proceed with the claim (if the judge accepts that you have an arguable case);

    b. to refuse permission (if the judge considers the claim unarguable);

    c. to refuse permission and certify the claim as "totally without merit" (if the judge considers the claim to be hopeless);

    d. to order that permission be considered at an oral hearing (if the judge is not sure whether the claim is arguable, and would like to hear oral argument on that point);

    e. to order that the question of permission be decided at a hearing, with the final hearing to follow immediately afterwards if permission is granted (this is often referred to as a 'rolled up/hearing'). An order of this sort is often made in cases that the judge considers are too complicated to grant permission without a hearing but need to be heard and decided urgently.

41. If permission is refused, you have seven days to request that the decision be reconsidered at an oral hearing, unless the case has been certified as totally without merit, in which case the claim cannot proceed further.

42. If permission is refused at an oral hearing (or the case is certified as totally without merit when permission is refused on the papers), a written application can be made to the Court of Appeal for permission to appeal within seven days of refusal. If the Court of Appeal refuses permission to appeal against the refusal of permission to apply for judicial review, that is the end of your case.

The final hearing

43. If permission to apply for judicial review is granted, the case will go to a final hearing.

44. When granting permission, a judge will usually give directions as to how the case will progress to the substantive hearing, including:

    a. the time within which the defendant or interested party or parties should file Detailed Grounds of Resistance and any evidence on which it is intended to rely at the hearing (usually 35 days). This is where the Defendant sets out in detail the basis on which they are defending the decision.

    b. which kind of judge should hear the case, and specifically whether it is suitable to be heard by a deputy judge or should be heard by a Divisional Court (a court with two or more judges), as to which see para 14.3 of this Guide;

    c. other case management directions including a timetable for skeleton arguments, trial bundles and authorities bundles to be lodged.

45. The matter will be set down for a full hearing. The full hearing is very formal. It involves lawyers from both sides making arguments about the lawfulness of the decision, act or failure to act which you have challenged. It is very unlikely you will have to give oral

evidence, and you may not even need to attend the hearing, unless you would like to do so for your own interest.

46. At the end of the hearing the judge can give judgment there and then, but that is unusual. The judge usually "reserves" the judgment, which means that the judgment will be given later, usually a few weeks after the hearing has taken place.

47. Once judgment is given then both sides can make representations about who should pay the costs of the proceedings. As explained below, the usual order is that the loser pays the winner's costs.

Particular issues which arise in the context of judicial review claims for asylum support

Pre-JR (pre action stage)

48. As noted earlier, the pre-action protocol for judicial review sets out a code of good practice and contains the steps which parties should generally follow before making a claim for judicial review. However, the protocol does also recognise that it will not be "appropriate in very urgent cases. In this sort of case, a claim should be made immediately"[48].

49. Asylum support cases can often fall into this category of very urgent cases. Common examples of this will be an asylum-seeker who is currently receiving section 95 support, but has been placed in accommodation which is having a severe and detrimental effect on his mental health. Or perhaps, a failed asylum seeker, who is being evicted from his current accommodation in a couple of days, and is in need of section 4(2) support immediately.

[48] Civil Procedure Rules, Practice Direction 54A

50. In these circumstances, complying with the pre-action protocol for judicial review is simply impractical due to the urgency of the individual's situation.

Permission stage

51. Who are your parties: As outlined earlier, in order to have standing in judicial review proceedings, it is necessary to have sufficient interest in the matter under challenge. For the purposes of an application for asylum support, it is quite clear to see how an applicant and their dependants to any application would have a sufficient interest. It is common in judicial review claims for, the applicant, spouse and children to all be included as claimants.

52. Anonymity: In cases relating to asylum support, it is notable that the Claimant in question is an asylum seeker. It is necessary to consider whether an application for anonymity should be sought pursuant to CPR r. 39.2(4) that their identity must not be disclosed and their name should be anonymised in the proceedings. The justification may be that the anonymity order is sought as, in the course of the Claimant's asylum claim, any Tribunal appeal would be subject to an order for anonymity. That protection which is afforded to asylum claimants should not be compromised by these proceedings. A further point is that the Claimant's Article 8 ECHR rights outweigh any media interest in this matter, and therefore any relevant rights under Article 10 ECHR. An Order would therefore meet the guidance given by the Supreme Court in *Re Guardian News and Media Ltd. [2010] 2 AC 697.*

Interim relief and urgent applications:

53. In judicial review claims, it is not uncommon for parties to seek interim relief. The reason for this is that like most litigation, judicial review proceedings can be lengthy and the final determination of a claim will often not be in the near future. Consequently, it may be

appropriate to seek an interim remedy due to the particular circumstances of the Claimant. That is to say: an order pending the final resolution of the judicial review claim.

54. Interim relief is usually requested in the Claim Form, but an application for it can be made at any stage of proceedings. Exceptionally, an application for interim relief may be made before starting judicial review proceedings. The Court may only grant an interim order before the claim has been issued where the matter is urgent or it is otherwise necessary to do so in the interests of justice. Alternatively, interim relief applications may be made when the claim is filed or after proceedings have been commenced.

55. When considering whether to grant interim relief while a judicial review claim is pending, the judge will consider whether there is a real issue to be tried and whether the balance of convenience lies in favour of granting the interim order. This involves balancing the harm to the claimant that would be caused if interim relief is not granted and the claim later succeeds against the harm to the defendant, any third parties and the public interest that would be caused if interim relief is granted and the claim later fails.

56. Seeking interim relief in the area of asylum support is very common. This is because by its very nature, applicants for asylum support are in need of adequate support straightaway as they will not have access to alternative support. Applicants will suffer great prejudice if they have to wait until the final determination of a claim.

57. On the question of whether there is a serious issue to be tried, it will often suffice to refer to the Statements of Facts and Grounds and rely on the matters argued as demonstrating the underlying merits of the case.

58. In reality, these matters are often determined on where the balance of convenience lies. In asylum support cases, the following issues will be relevant to determining where the balance of convenience lies:

a. Are there children involved?

b. Is the Applicant or dependant pregnant?

c. Does the Applicant or dependant have a medical condition – physical or mental health?

d. Does the accommodation have a negative effect on the medical condition?

e. Does the Applicant or Dependant have sufficient connections in a particular area in the UK?

CHAPTER FOUR

KEY RECENT JUDGMENTS IN THE AREA OF ASYLUM SUPPORT

R (HA and Ors) v SSHD[49]

Summary

1. Five linked JR claims, all of which concern the SSHD's obligations under the Immigration and Asylum Act 1999 ("the 1999 Act") and the Asylum Support Regulations 2000 ("the 2000 Regulations"), to provide accommodation and support to meet the essential living needs of asylum seekers.

Context

2. The facts giving rise to each claim occurred in 2021 and 2022. The asylum support system was (and is still) operating under the significant pressure and strain that had developed during the pandemic period.

3. What this meant in practice:

    - Delays in Home Office decision-making.

    - Lack of dispersal accommodation.

---

49 [2023] EWHC 1876 (Admin)

- Growing backlog of asylum claims and asylum support applications.

4. Net effect: Over-reliance on initial accommodation (i.e., hotels)

Issues

- **Issue 1:** K and NY complained that the SSHD had failed to decide their section 95 applications promptly (breach of section 95 obligation).

- **Issue 2:** NY complained that the SSHD agreed to provide section 95 support but then there was significant delay in receiving support for several months (breach of section 95 obligation).

- **Issue 3:** K and NY additionally complained that the SSHD had acted unlawfully by failing to provide her with financial support to meet essential living needs pursuant to section 98, pending the decision on her section 95 application (breach of section 98 obligation).

- **Issue 4:** HA and SXK complained whether additional support the SSHD must provide to pregnant women and children under 3 years old, by reason of Regulation 10A of the 2000 Regulations, must be given by way of the cash payment referred to in regulation 10A, or whether the obligation under that regulation can be discharged by provision in kind.

Issue 1

5. *K*: Section 95 application made in January 2022. On 8 August 2022, K was informed her application had been granted. At the hearing SSHD conceded that there had been unreasonable delay.

6. *NY*: Section 95 application made in March 2021. On 27 May 2021, application was granted.

7. It was held that the delay in deciding *K* and *NY's* applications for s.95 support was unreasonable and incompatible with the Home Secretary's duty/obligation to decide an application "promptly" under the 1999 Act and 2000 regs.

8. See [35], [37-38], [48] and [63]. Paragraph [37] of the judgment is particularly relevant:

> *"the obligation to take section 95 decisions promptly cannot be equated to a set period of time that applies in all cases [...] what promptness requires for this purpose is that section 95 applications are decided by the Home Secretary within a short period following an applicant's first contact with Migrant Help. [...]. In all cases the Home Secretary and those she has contracted with must act promptly; in most cases a decision ought to be taken within 10 days"*[50].

9. **Consequences:** a section 95 eligibility decision **ought to be taken within 10 days from initial contact with Migrant Help**. Failure to do this will most likely mean that the SSHD has acted unlawfully under the 1999 Act and 2000 Regulations.

Issue 2

10. *NY:* From section 95 decision grant on 27 May 2021, the SSHD failed to provide any support until 22 December 2021. It was held that this was a further breach of the SSHD's obligations under the 1999 Act and 2000 regulations.

---

[50] [2023] EWHC 1876 (Admin) at para 37

11. See [49-51]. Paragraph [49] states:

> *"Neither the Act nor the Regulations prescribes the period within which section 95 support is to commence once a decision to provide that support has been made. However, given the nature of a section 95 decision, which is an acceptance that the applicant is, or is soon to be, destitute, the necessary inference is that once a decision has been made steps towards making section 95 provision will start immediately and will be pursued efficiently. Each case will therefore turn on its own facts.*[51] *"*

Consequences: No prescribed period of time, however, is 14 days from grant a useful benchmark? (See reg 7 of 2000 regulations). In this case, the court concluded that *NY's* support should have been forthcoming from mid-June 2021.

It will turn on the individual facts of each case. Relevant factors: Pregnant asylum seeker, mental/physical health needs, children.

<u>Issue 3</u>

12. *NY*: It was held that the SSHD failed to meet her obligations to provide section 98 temporary support in the form of payments to meet essential living needs.

13. The SSHD had admitted that such payments had been made prior to 2017. Since 2017, SSHD only provides hotel accommodation in exercise of section 98 (initial accommodation).

14. The paragraphs which are of particular importance are [41-45] and [51]. Paragraph 51 states as follows:

[51] [2023] EWHC 1876 (Admin) at para 49

> *"It is obvious there will be occasions where the provision of support for essential living needs outside accommodation provided by the Home Secretary better suits the circumstances of the applicant"*[52].

15. **Consequences:** Asylum seekers can apply for temporary financial support under section 98 whether or not they are in initial accommodation (i.e. asylum seeker may apply from private accommodation) if there are delays in processing section 95 applications.

16. When is the right time to make an application for s.98 financial support? Fact-sensitive! E.g. private accommodation host does not have necessary means to financially support?

Issue 4

17. *HA* and *SXK* succeeded on their primary submission that from the time they should have received support under section 95 of the 1999 Act, they should have received the payment specified in regulation 10A. The SSHD is not permitted to discharge the obligation under regulation 10A by provision of support in kind.

18. The implication of this is that the £3 top-up payment to pregnant mothers under Reg 10A must be paid in cash.

19. Relevant paragraphs are [13-18] of the judgment.

20. **Consequences:** There will be many *legacy* cases. Representations should be made for the SSHD to reconsider any pre-*HA* Reg 10A refusals in light of the *HA* judgment.

---

52 [2023] EWHC 1876 (Admin) at para 51

Relief = Backdated Payments. SSHD should make backdated payments from date of application. This can be sought on the following grounds:

- Declaratory relief (failure to pay under reg 10A unlawful) and compensatory damages for a sum due;
- Alternatively, declaratory relief (failure to pay under reg 10A unlawful) and damages in restitution in respect of backdated payments;
- Rely on SSHD's 'Conditions of Support' policy, dated 2 March 2023

R (SA) v SSHD[53]

Summary

21. The Claimant was a destitute asylum seeker. She was heavily pregnant and had 3 other young children. They were accommodated by SSHD in initial accommodation, first at a hotel in Croydon, and then a hotel in Peckham. The case challenged the adequacy of the accommodation and the SSHD's failure to relocate the Claimant to subsequent dispersal accommodation. The Claimant was successful, with Fordham J finding that the SSHD had breached the statutory duty owed to the Claimant and her children.

---

[53] [2023] EWHC 1787 (Admin)

Context

22. Almost the same legislation applied in this case as *HA*.

23. Additional key consideration in this case was the SSHD's Healthcare Needs and Pregnancy Dispersal Policy.

24. Involves initial accommodation provided under s.98 IAA 1999, s.95 support then being granted, but hotel accommodation, albeit a different hotel, is then provided pursuant to s.95 IAA 1999. The period of time concerned about was the total time at each hotel, amounting to 15 months.

25. A very useful judgment consolidating matters raised and established in various cases. Paragraph [1] of the judgment helpfully sets out the relevant legislation, policy, and line of authorities.

Issues

26. **Issue 1:** Reinforcing the twin-track test established in *R (NB) v SSHD* [2021] EWHC 1489 (Admin) [2021]; (§§ 161 and 171);

27. **Issue 2:** Cumulative effect of multiple inadequacy issues;

28. **Issue 3:** Importance of Healthcare Needs and Pregnancy Dispersal Policy to support a breach on each of the two tracks;

29. **Issue 4**: Lack of evidence served by the SSHD.

Issue 1

30. Twin-track test to establish if the SSHD has discharged her statutory duty was well established in *NB* (§§154-155 and 161). Fordham J

re-emphasised that this test applies to adequacy of accommodation at paragraph [8]:

a. *First part of the twin-track = does the SSHD's response meet an* ***'objective minimum standard'****?*

b. *Second part of the twin-track test = does the SSHD's response involve an* ***evaluative judgment which is reasonable****?*

31. Paragraph [11]:

> *"I have concluded, applying the twin track test (NB §161), that there is a breach on each track (as in NB at §171), <u>either of which suffices</u>"*[54] in the sense that Fordham J could find that the SSHD had breached her statutory obligation to the Claimant.

32. **<u>Consequences:</u>** continues to be essential to apply the twin-track test established in *NB*, but *SA* now provides an additional key authority as to the applicability of the twin-track test.

Issue 2

33. Critically, Fordham J was clear that in finding there was a breach of statutory duty and that the SSHD's view was unreasonable, it was "*the* ***combination of features*** *which have led me to those conclusions*"; [11].

34. Helpfully, the relevant factors were identified individually, and they totalled 8 separate factors; pregnancy and vulnerability (§§12-14), the baby (§15), the room (§16), somewhere to eat (§17), somewhere

[54] [2023] EWHC 1787 (Admin) at para 11

for homework (§18), somewhere to play (§19), passage of time (§§20-22), and open-ended uncertainty (§23).

35. Importance of passage of time was emphasised at [20]: "*I come to the feature of the case which – when put alongside the other features –* ***becomes decisive.***" Fordham J specifically addressed in the same paragraph "*that accommodation can have been legally adequate for a shorter timeframe but cannot satisfy the tests of legal adequacy in the longer term*".

36. Cumulative effect is specifically dealt with at [24] – "*It is the* ***cumulative effect of all of these features*** *that leave me with confidence to conclude that this is a case in which the Home Secretary is in present breach of her statutory duty.*"[55]

37. **Consequences:** key that there has to be a combination of various features, some of which are of more significance (passage of time in this case) than others, to amount to a breach of statutory duty.

Issue 3

38. Found that there had been an "***unjustified departure from applicable Policy*** *– as a matter of both process and substance*"[56].

39. This Policy contains specific guidance in relation to the needs of pregnant applicants. This Policy continues to be in force, and so in similar cases of pregnant women, or women who have very recently given birth, it is essential this Policy is included in the Statement of Facts and Grounds.

---

[55] [2023] EWHC 1787 (Admin) at para 24

[56] [2023] EWHC 1787 (Admin) at para 12

40. Re-emphasises the need to set out cases of *Mandalia v Secretary of State for the Home Department* [2015] 1 WLR 4546, para 31 per Lord Wilson; *R (Lee-Hirons) v Secretary of State for Justice* [2016] UKSC 46; [2017] AC 52, para 17 per Lord Wilson. Both of which set out that the SSHD is under a duty to follow the Guidance, unless she identifies a good reason for not doing so during the course of the decision-making process

Issue 4

41. The SSHD essentially filed no evidence, other than a very late witness statement in this case, and the significance of this was made abundantly clear by Fordham J at [26] which deals specifically with the SSHD's decision-making and record keeping. A key passage is the following:

> "*There was ample opportunity to file evidence, under the right in CPR54 and the directions of the Court, alongside a pleaded defence. That opportunity was not taken. A choice was made. The failure to engage by demonstrating and evidencing any evaluative decision-making can have practical consequences when the Court comes to grapple with the legality of the way in which a statutory function has been approached. There is a limit to the extent to which submissions – as opposed to evidenced decision-making – can successfully invoke the latitude built into the public law standards of reasonableness review…*".[57]

42. **<u>Consequences:</u>** Seems to be a recurring theme in cases at the moment, where the SSHD is not filing evidence at any point during proceedings, and if they do so, it is just before a substantive hearing.

---

57 [2023] EWHC 1787 (Admin) at para 26

43. Possibility of utilising CPR18, a request for further information, if the SSHD asserts that enquiries have been made, or makes assertions about accommodation which are not substantiated. If they do not comply, this can be determined by the Court and will have cost consequences for the SSHD.

MORE BOOKS BY LAW BRIEF PUBLISHING

A selection of our other titles available now:-

'A Practical Guide to Probation Breaches and Other Applications' by Mark Thomas
'A Practical Guide to Remarriage and Divorce' by Cordelia Williams & Claire Howard
'A Practical Guide to Privacy, Transparency, Reporting Restrictions and Closed Proceedings in the Court of Protection' by Laura Mannering
'Beaumont on Barristers – A Guide to Defending Disciplinary Proceedings (Second Edition)' by Marc Beaumont
'A Practical Guide to Payments for Environmental Services' by Ben Sharples
'A Practical Guide to the Law of Pregnancy and Maternity at Work' by Rebecca Thomas
'A Practical Guide to Redundancy – Second Edition' by Philip Hyland & Collette Moore
'A Practical Guide to International Issues for Scottish Family Lawyers' by Susie Mountain, Donna McKay, Ken MacDonald
'A Practical Guide to the Law on Deprivation of Liberty' by Ben Troke
'A Practical Guide to Rights over Airspace and Subsoil – Second Edition' by Daniel Gatty
'A Practical Guide to the Law in Relation to Inquests' by Ramya Nagesh
'A Practical Guide to the Construction and Rectification of Wills and Trust Instruments (Second Edition)' by Edward Hewitt
'A Practical Guide to Data Protection in Social Housing' by Clare Paterson
'A Practical Guide to Spousal Maintenance – Second Edition' by Liz Cowell
'A Practical Guide to International Parental Child Abduction Law (England and Wales)' by Dr Onyója Momoh
'A Practical Guide to Deprivation of British Citizenship' by Sean Ell
'A Practical Guide to Commercial Property Service Charges' by Rachel Garton
'A Practical Guide to Clinical Negligence – Third Edition' by Geoffrey Simpson-Scott (Geoff)
'A Practical Guide to the Rights of Grandparents in Children Proceedings – Second Edition' by Stuart Barlow

'The Electronic Communications Code: A Practical Guide – Second Edition' by Kerry Bretherton KC, James Castle, Mark Loveday
'A Practical Guide to the Independent School Standards – September 2023 Edition' by Sarah McKimm
'A Practical Guide to Estate Administration and Crypto Assets' by Richard Marshall
'A Practical Guide to Parental Alienation in Private and Public Law Children Cases' by Sam King QC & Frankie Shama
'Contested Heritage – Removing Art from Land and Historic Buildings' by Richard Harwood QC, Catherine Dobson, David Sawtell
'The Limits of Separate Legal Personality: When Those Running a Company Can Be Held Personally Liable for Losses Caused to Third Parties Outside of the Company' by Dr Mike Wilkinson
'A Practical Guide to Transgender Law' by Robin Moira White & Nicola Newbegin
'A Practical Guide to 'Stranded Spouses' in Family Law' by Mani Singh Basi
'A Practical Guide to Residential Freehold Conveyancing' by Lorraine Richardson
'A Practical Guide to Pensions on Divorce for Lawyers' by Bryan Scant
'A Practical Guide to Challenging Sham Marriage Allegations in Immigration Law' by Priya Solanki
'A Practical Guide to Digital Communications Evidence in Criminal Law' by Sam Willis
'A Practical Guide to Legal Rights in Scotland' by Sarah-Jane Macdonald
'A Practical Guide to New Build Conveyancing' by Paul Sams & Rebecca East
'A Practical Guide to Inherited Wealth on Divorce' by Hayley Trim
'A Practical Guide to Practice Direction 12J and Domestic Abuse in Private Law Children Proceedings' by Rebecca Cross & Malvika Jaganmohan
'A Practical Guide to Confiscation and Restraint' by Narita Bahra QC, John Carl Townsend, David Winch
'A Practical Guide to the Law of Forests in Scotland' by Philip Buchan
'A Practical Guide to Health and Medical Cases in Immigration Law' by Rebecca Chapman & Miranda Butler
'A Practical Guide to Bad Character Evidence for Criminal Practitioners by Aparna Rao
'A Practical Guide to Extradition Law post-Brexit' by Myles Grandison et al
'A Practical Guide to Hoarding and Mental Health for Housing Lawyers' by Rachel Coyle

'Stephens on Contractual Indemnities' by Richard Stephens
'A Practical Guide to the EU Succession Regulation' by Richard Frimston
'A Practical Guide to Solicitor and Client Costs – Second Edition' by Robin Dunne
'Constructive Dismissal – Practice Pointers and Principles' by Benjimin Burgher
'A Practical Guide to Religion and Belief Discrimination Claims in the Workplace' by Kashif Ali
'A Practical Guide to the Law of Medical Treatment Decisions' by Ben Troke
'Fundamental Dishonesty and QOCS in Personal Injury Proceedings: Law and Practice' by Jake Rowley
'A Practical Guide to the Law in Relation to School Exclusions' by Charlotte Hadfield & Alice de Coverley
'A Practical Guide to Divorce for the Silver Separators' by Karin Walker
'The Right to be Forgotten – The Law and Practical Issues' by Melissa Stock
'A Practical Guide to Planning Law and Rights of Way in National Parks, the Broads and AONBs' by James Maurici QC, James Neill et al
'A Practical Guide to Election Law' by Tom Tabori
'A Practical Guide to the Law in Relation to Surrogacy' by Andrew Powell
'A Practical Guide to Claims Arising from Fatal Accidents – Second Edition' by James Patience
'A Practical Guide to Asbestos Claims' by Jonathan Owen & Gareth McAloon
'A Practical Guide to Stamp Duty Land Tax in England and Northern Ireland' by Suzanne O'Hara
'A Practical Guide to the Law of Farming Partnerships' by Philip Whitcomb
'A Practical Guide to the Law of Unlawful Eviction and Harassment – Second Edition' by Stephanie Lovegrove
'A Practical Guide to Costs in Personal Injury Claims – Second Edition' by Matthew Hoe
'A Practical Guide to the General Data Protection Regulation (GDPR) – Second Edition' by Keith Markham
'A Practical Guide to Working with Litigants in Person and McKenzie Friends in Family Cases' by Stuart Barlow
'Protecting Unregistered Brands: A Practical Guide to the Law of Passing Off' by Lorna Brazell
'A Practical Guide to Secondary Liability and Joint Enterprise Post-Jogee' by Joanne Cecil & James Mehigan

'A Practical Guide to the Pre-Action RTA Claims Protocol for Personal Injury Lawyers' by Antonia Ford
'A Practical Guide to Neighbour Disputes and the Law' by Alexander Walsh
'A Practical Guide to Coercive Control for Legal Practitioners and Victims' by Rachel Horman
'A Practical Guide to the Law of Driverless Cars – Second Edition'
by Alex Glassbrook, Emma Northey & Scarlett Milligan
'A Practical Guide to TOLATA Claims' by Greg Williams
'A Practical Guide to Elderly Law – Second Edition' by Justin Patten
'A Practical Guide to Responding to Housing Disrepair and Unfitness Claims' by Iain Wightwick
'A Practical Guide to the Law of Bullying and Harassment in the Workplace' by Philip Hyland
'How to Be a Freelance Solicitor: A Practical Guide to the SRA-Regulated Freelance Solicitor Model' by Paul Bennett
'A Practical Guide to Prison Injury Claims' by Malcolm Johnson
'A Practical Guide to Advising Clients at the Police Station' by Colin Stephen McKeown-Beaumont
'A Practical Guide to Antisocial Behaviour Injunctions – Second Edition' by Iain Wightwick
'Practical Mediation: A Guide for Mediators, Advocates, Advisers, Lawyers, and Students in Civil, Commercial, Business, Property, Workplace, and Employment Cases' by Jonathan Dingle with John Sephton
'The Mini-Pupillage Workbook' by David Boyle
'A Practical Guide to Crofting Law' by Brian Inkster
'A Practical Guide to the Law of Domain Names and Cybersquatting' by Andrew Clemson
'A Practical Guide to the Law of Gender Pay Gap Reporting' by Harini Iyengar
'NHS Whistleblowing and the Law' by Joseph England
'Employment Law and the Gig Economy' by Nigel Mackay & Annie Powell
'A Practical Guide to Noise Induced Hearing Loss (NIHL) Claims' by Andrew Mckie, Ian Skeate, Gareth McAloon
'An Introduction to Beauty Negligence Claims – A Practical Guide for the Personal Injury Practitioner' by Greg Almond
'Intercompany Agreements for Transfer Pricing Compliance' by Paul Sutton
'Zen and the Art of Mediation' by Martin Plowman
'A Practical Guide to Adoption for Family Lawyers' by Graham Pegg

www.ingramcontent.com/pod-product-compliance
Lightning Source LLC
LaVergne TN
LVHW022304200926
848481LV00004B/1212
* 9 7 8 1 9 1 6 6 9 8 6 6 6 *